Have a Word With God

Other books by Dr. Hutchison:

THE CHURCH AND SPIRITUAL HEALING	Rider & Co., 1955
A FAITH TO LIVE BY	W. A. Wilde, USA, 1959
SCOTTISH PUBLIC EDUCATIONAL DOCUMENTS	S.C.R.E., 1973
KIRK LIFE IN OLD CARMUNNOCK	Carmunnock Kirk Session, 1978
GOD BELIEVES IN YOU!	Eyre & Spottiswoode, 1980
CARMUNNOCK CHURCH, 1854 – 1948	Carmunnock Kirk Session, 1980
WELL, I'M BLESSED!	Eyre & Spottiswoode, 1981
HEALING THROUGH WORSHIP	Eyre & Spottiswoode, 1981

Have A Word With God

Original Prayers
for Personal use

by

HARRY HUTCHISON

First published in 1981 by
Eyre & Spottiswoode (Publishers) Ltd.
North Way, Andover, Hampshire SP10 5BE

ISBN 0 413 80200 0
Printed by T. J. Press (Padstow) Ltd.
Padstow, Cornwall

CONTENTS

Dr. Henry Hutchison was born in Alloa, Clackmannanshire, and attended Dollar Academy where he was Athletics Champion as well as Dux Medallist. For a few years he played cricket for Clackmannan County. After a period of War Service in the Royal Air Force, he completed his M.A. and B.D. Degrees at Edinburgh University, and later gained the B.Ed. of Toronto University and the M.Litt. and Ph.D. Degrees of Glasgow University. He is a trained teacher and holds Diplomas in Music and in Religious Education.

His first charge as a Minister of the Church of Scotland was in Saltcoats, Ayrshire. He moved to Glasgow for a few years before accepting a Call to St. Paul's Presbyterian Church, Peterborough, Ontario—one of the largest Presbyterian congregations in Canada. On returning to Scotland he became involved in the teaching of religion in schools, but in 1967 he was appointed Lecturer in Education at Glasgow University.

Eventually deciding to move back into parish work, he was inducted to the historic parish of Carmunnock in 1977. He has contributed to many Journals—several of his articles and sermons, for example, having appeared in the *Expository Times* and in *The Christian Ministry* (USA)—and the titles of some of his books are noted elsewhere in the present volume. He is married, with one son who holds a Major Open Scholarship at Oxford.

FOREWORD

George Meredith once said that 'Who rises from prayer a better man, his prayer is answered'. Now it's easy for the Christian to become a little perturbed at the suggestion that prayer is a purely subjective thing, but perhaps we ought not to dismiss entirely the *partial* truth which Meredith had grasped. What I mean is this: that although prayer is, of course, the expression of a faith that already exists, may it not be *also* an 'instrument' for producing a better person?

This little book of original prayers, written in modern format, is sent out in the conviction that prayer is not only something to be enjoyed, and is not only the natural expression of things deeply felt, but is also an activity which leads to the deepening of faith and life—particularly if it is practised regularly.

Whether or not 'he who ceases to pray ceases to prosper', as the proverb asserts, it is certainly true that the person who doesn't pray is missing one of the loveliest and one of the most sublime experiences open to men and women. 'HAVE A WORD WITH GOD.' That's sound advice! For, as the Christian believes, we were made for communion with God.

There is of course no necessity to use the prayers in the order in which they come in this book, though this is certainly one way of using them. Whatever order is found best, the material is designed to be sufficient for a period of three months. May those who use this book as an aid to 'having a word with God' find that 'the Lord's ears *are* open to their prayers'!

H.H.

The Manse of Carmunnock,
by Glasgow.
January, 1981

GOD THE CREATOR

I

Each new day, O God,
you renew the miracle of creation—
but how easily I become blind to it!
Heavenly Father, open my eyes anew
to the wonder of your creation.
May the movement of the cloud and the song of the
bird speak to me of your love and providence.
I rejoice, O God,
in the air I breathe and the life I live,
in the blessing of family and friends,
in the fine influences and interests of life.

O you who are my maker and sustainer,
I acknowledge afresh that you are worthy
of my worship and my praise.
You are the giver of all I am and have.
Without your creating love and power
I could not know the blessing of being alive.
You have set me in this world, Lord,
to find its beauty and to enjoy it—
and especially to enjoy you, the creator.
You have made me so that I can respond
to everything that is good and true—
especially the good and truth that you are.

O creator and Lord, you who give me
the power to see your glory around me,
in the earth and in the sky,
in the faces of my fellows,
let me always remember that you are not only my
creator, but my Lord and my Redeemer as well!
And may others know it by the way I live!
Amen.

II

O God, the loving creator of all things,
what a wonderful world you have made!
Season succeeds to season, night to day,
cold to warmth, barrenness to fruitfulness.

Lord Christ, give me eyes
to see what is holiest and best.
Lord Christ, give me ears
to hear the loveliest harmonies of creation.
Lord Christ, give me lips
to tell what I have seen and heard.

Set as I am, O God,
in a world of great beauty—
one which speaks to me
of your love and power and glory,
and remembering especially the season
which brings before us
the miracle of your re-creating love,
I pray you, Lord, to nourish my soul
as the soil nourishes the life of creation.
Turn the winter of our lives
into the the springtime of hope and happiness,
and may your love so warm my heart
that I may be drawn towards you
as flowers to the sun.
Let me find true purity of heart,
and so enjoy a vision of you, O God.
Forgive me, Lord, when I have been blind
to the wonder of your world,
and oblivious to my status
as a creature of your love and care.
Now help me better to appreciate
both the simple things of life
and the wonders of your creation—
and to you I shall give the praise! Amen.

III

What an abundance of gifts I receive
at your hand, O God!
You ripen the grain for my daily bread.
You cause the sun to shine.
You bring the refreshing rain.
Hill and valley, cloud and sea,
are all your creation, O God,
and I revel in their beauty!

Your creative power, Lord, is no less
if men think they are untouched by it.
Your reign is no less real
if men are blind to your majesty.
But as for me, Lord, I praise you afresh
for the numberless joys and comforts
of this life on earth,
and for the insight to see this world
as a sign of your power and majesty.
In so many marvellous ways, Lord,
you have enriched my life—
and not least by the basic necessities
of ordinary living.
For food and shelter, books and hobbies,
friends to meet and a job to do,
I praise you, creator God!

Help me, Lord, to find joy and satisfaction
in simple and homely things,
while realising that my chief enriching
comes not from anything external,
but from your inner presence.
And now, I pray, continue your creative work
in me, that I may reflect at least a little
of your great glory.

Amen.

IV

O Lord my God, your glory flames
not only from sun and star,
but from human hearts
fired by an utter dedication to yourself.
Let my heart be one of them, Lord!
And now, O God, for everything
that is lovely and awe-inspiring
in your creation I praise you.
Praise be yours for the silent message
that comes to my heart and mind
from sun and moon and star.
Praise be yours for the silver glory of water
and the golden glory of the sunrise;
for the billowy clouds;
for the song of the birds.
May I become possessed, O my creator,
by a sense of utter and joyful wonder
at the majesty and magnificence of your world.
Forbid that I shall ever take for granted
the good things that come from your hand—
but let my soul exult in God my creator!

Almighty God, I know you have created me
and breathed into me the breath of life,
and I am humbled by this amazing gift
of an immortal soul.
Into that which is material
you have infused that which is spiritual—
and there is no miracle of man's
which is as wonderful as that!
Just grant, O Lord, that I may never refuse
to rise to the heights for which I am made.
'Breathe on me, breath of God,
And fill me with life anew'! Amen.

V

We all like receiving gifts, O God!
And how grateful I am for the gifts
  of health and home, of earth's beauty,
  of great music, and of blue skies.
Lord, they are all from your hand.

Eternal and all-powerful God,
  'Thou who mad'st the atom's hidden forces,
  Whose laws its mighty energies fulfil',
I praise you today with glad abandon
  that all things—and all men—
  were made through you, the Creator.
My heart is glad, O Lord my God,
  that you've revealed yourself so clearly—
  and so colourfully!—in the world you've made.
I live among so many splendours,
  and yet sometimes I am blind to them.
Let me, Lord, be far more grateful
  for the gifts of your hand.

And in praising you now, O creator God,
  for making me what I am,
  I pray you to help me come to terms
  with my creatureliness.
Let your creative spirit work unceasingly
  to overcome the disorder and dispeace
  that is within me.
And when I seem to be drawing a veil
  across your glory,
  let that glory continue to break through!
Now give me your life, Lord,
  so that nothing may be too much for me
  to attempt for you, and so that I may have the joy
  of having a part in your creative purposes.

Amen.

VI

How majestic is your name, O God,
  in the world you have made!
For all the goodness which surrounds me
  I rejoice and thank you, Lord.
And I am glad to have eyes
  which *can* see you in your creation,
  for I know how much this adds
  to the richness of men's lives.
And if I am thankful for the beauty of the world,
  I am even more thankful for yourself,
  and for the sense of wellbeing
  which your creative spirit has induced in me.
May I realise afresh that your desire
  is to make me more like yourself,
  to 'polish up' the image of yourself
  which is within me
  and which has so often
  become faded and tarnished.

By your gifts may I live, Lord.
By your breath may I breathe, Lord.
By your light may I walk, Lord.

O God, your never-failing providence
  is a source of constant wonder to me.
You have not only created all things,
  but you uphold and sustain them—and me!
And let me be quite sure that you are the one
    'Who stamped thine image on thy
      creatures,
    And although they marred that image,
          lov'st them still'.

Amen.

VII

I praise you today, creator God, that you are
 'Life, awaking life in cell and tissue,
 From flower to bird,
 From beast to brain of man'.
For the wonder and beauty of your world,
 I give you praise, O God.
Give me, Lord, clearer eyes
 to see this your loveliness,
 and a sharper mind to appreciate it better.
May some of the calm content of nature be mine.
May I absorb something of her serenity.
May my life show something of her beauty.

It's your sun that ripened the golden grain,
 but bread's getting more and more expensive.
So are all the necessities of life.
But food for the soul is still the same price.
 It's priceless.
May men desire it more.
May they receive it thankfully from your hand.
 'We taste thee, O thou living bread,
 And long to feast upon thee still.'

And now may I never cease to praise you
 for the miracle by which my life is sustained.
May I praise you not only for the warmth of the sun
 but for Him who is sun of my soul.
May I praise you not only for refreshing rain
 but for your 'still dews of quietness'.
May I praise you not only for the beauty of sky
 but for that
 'country far beyond the stars
 where stands a winged sentry'.

Amen.

THE WORD OF GOD

I

Your word, O God, isn't held prisoner
  by the covers of a sacred book!
Nor is its meaning exhausted
  by those who preach and teach it.
Let me, O Christ, regularly expose myself
  to your Word, written and preached—
  but fill me with the glad knowledge
  that I see it best in YOU,
  and in the deeds of your followers today!
Your word is living and active.
And *my* life and *my* action are for you!

I praise you now, Lord,
  for the incisiveness and power of your word,
  and for quickening *my* heart and mind by it.
I now know the joy of living 'in Christ'!
Daily, Lord, we are surfeited and bombarded
  by the words of man.
Newspapers, hoardings, journals, books.
Radio, television, theatre, film.
Some of it edifies; much of it doesn't.

O Lord, we desperately need your word—
  to edify, to challenge, to evangelise,
  to bring hope and *good* news, for a change!
There are few things, Lord, that I want
  more than to hear and answer your word.
My heart *is* open to your truth.
But let it find fresh entrance into me today.
And let me always remember, Lord,
  that it's your word, not my works,
  which saves me!

Amen.

II

'We must pay closer attention
  to what we have heard',
  says an Epistle writer—and I know
  it's sound advice, Lord!
So much goes in one ear and out the other!
And it's true, sometimes, of your Word!
In the life of each day, O living Word,
  I could be so much more careful
  putting into practice what I've heard
  about the Faith.

Forgive me where I have failed to pay
  closer attention to your word and my witness.
Give me a fresh resolve, O God,
  to amend what I have been.
Make me joyful at every sign of your coming,
  and let me pay somewhat closer attention
  to these signs and to their personal challenge.

You, Lord, have a word for us all.
Where there is despair, bring the word of hope.
Where there is lifelessness, bring the word of life.
Where there is pain, bring the word of healing.
Let us all have the assurance
  that you go before us
  as we walk the pathways of life,
  and let us remember that
  all things are working together for good—
  but that only those who love you
  will be able to accept your word!
Lord, *I* love you, and so I can sing
    'Lord, thy word abideth,
    And our footsteps guideth'.

Amen.

III

Gracious God, I know your word to me
is more important than my word to you—
though you *do* want to hear from me, Lord!
Gladly I come to 'Have a Word with God'
and to listen to the divine voice.

For all the duties of life, O God,
I shall need strength.
For all the desires of life, O God,
I shall need purity.
For all the problems of life, O God,
I shall need wisdom.
And how better shall I find these things
than through him, the living Word,
the almighty, the all-pure, the all-wise one!
So in these days may your gracious word illumine for me the road that I shall take.

You, Lord, have given to all mankind
the word which spells life!
Let more people hear it, understand it,
and respond to it—even now.
And what of those, Lord, who *have* heard it
but have not taken firm enough hold on it?
Maybe I myself have read your word in the Bible,
or I've heard it preached,
or have seen it lived—
and have been only momentarily impressed!
Instead of holding *fast* the word of life,
I have sometimes held *back* from it.

Now grant that I may come to your word
in the renewed belief that it *will*
make a real difference to my living.
And may each day's pilgrimage bring me
a new experience of you, the very word of life!
Amen.

IV

Your own word, O God, claims
that you are above all gods—
and I really do believe it!
I know, of course, that many 'gods'
claim my allegiance, Lord—
power, money, success, popularity.
But in my heart of hearts I know
you are above all gods.
I am determined to rest in your power,
holding fast to the confidence that you will, as your word promises, preserve me until you have fulfilled the end for which you first created me.
I know from your word, O God,
that you can bring life out of death
and can create beauty out of desolation—
and I know from experience
that you can transform darkness into light!
I know from your word, O God,
that I am made in your image, able to link myself with the eternal—and I rejoice now that the personal link *has* been made, even though it may be somewhat tenuous!
You have taught me in your word, Lord,
to dread nothing but the loss of yourself.
So preserve me from needless fears
and from undue anxieties,
so that your love which is immortal
may shine out in all its splendour,
and my heart may be warmed in its rays.
And let me always remember that I live
not by bread alone, but by your word.
So may I listen more attentively to it,
and more zealously obey it.
For Jesus' sake. Amen.

V

Are your promises at an end for all time?
  asks the Psalmist.
What a rhetorical question, Lord!
The promises of your own word
  are the source of my hope, O God.
    'Tell out, my soul, the glories of his word.
    Firm is his promise, and his mercy sure.'

Grant me today, Lord, a full measure of faith
  to trust in the promises of your word—
  faith to trust my whole self to you;
  faith to leave every issue in your hands;
  faith to hope even when 'prospects' seem
    poor.

For the supreme revelation of yourself in Jesus
  I praise your name, O God.
O you who are the Word,
  I rejoice today in your goodness
  that you prompted men to set down in
    writing
  the very plan of salvation.
For all that the Bible means to me,
  I thank you, O God.
Praise be yours for him
  who is its chief character and sole inspiration.
May its pages leap into life
  as he fulfils them anew in *my* life!

For the story of Christ's incarnation
  and for his being born anew in me;
For the story of Christ's Cross
  and for its prompting me to fresh penitence;
For the story of Christ's resurrection
  and for my sharing in his risen power—
            I praise you, O God!

Amen.

VI

O you who have set me in a world
which seems to prize novelty and change,
let me always be ready to consider the new,
but let me also be sure of the wisdom
of holding to the traditions I was taught.
Your Word, Lord, never goes out of date,
but help me to apply it
with insight and resourcefulness
in the changing patterns of our daily lives.
The words you speak to me, O God,
are spirit and life—
but I could be much more 'spirited'
and full of life for you!
Yours, Lord, is the word of truth—
but sometimes I've been far too ready
to settle for half-truths.
Yours, Lord, is the word of peace—
but how seldom I ask you to take from my soul
all strain and stress
and to order my life that I may confess
the beauty of your peace!

But I do acknowledge, Lord,
that you caused your word to be written down
for my growth in grace,
and I pray that I may never look on the Bible
as a kind of 'extra' to Christian living,
or as a kind of 'status symbol'!
Grant, Lord, that in these days lying before me
it may truly be a lamp to my feet,
and a vivid reminder of the newness of life
in which I should be walking.
Through Him who is the Word.
Amen.

VII

Your word, O God, invites me daily
  to say 'Yes' to you.
And this I do—now!

Help me, spirit of wisdom,
  to understand your word of truth.
Help me, spirit of pardon,
  to accept your word of peace.
Help me, spirit of grace,
  to cherish your word of hope.

You speak to us in love, O God,
  so that we may live without fear.
I know from your word
  what your purpose is for me.
You desire to give me life—real life!
You seek my wholeness.
Let me, then, be ever desirous
  of becoming a *new* person
  rather than being a 'nice' person!
As I ponder the glory and challenge of your word,
  and of Him who is the Word,
  grant that I may always be ready
  to seek courage before escape,
  to think of others before self,
  to follow Christ rather than my inclinations.

Through your word, Lord, let all men
  find light to guide them through life.
Let them rejoice—as I do—
  that your mercy is greater than our folly;
  that your love is more important than our pride.
And grant that I may always
  have that healthy perspective
  which stresses the promises of your word
  more than the feelings of my heart!   Amen.

CONFESSION

I

You have the power and the desire to forgive me,
O Christ; and I am separated from you only by my pretence or my pride.
I bring my confession to you now,
knowing my daily life cannot 'go right'
if I have not 'got right' with you.
So forgive me the shortcomings
which have grieved you and disgraced me—
and make me more conscious of them.

I confess, O Lord, those times
when I had the chance of working for you
but chose to do nothing;
when I had the chance of 'growing' for you
but chose to 'wither up';
when I had the chance of standing up for Jesus
but chose to stand on ceremony!
Forgive me and strengthen me, O Lord.

Receive the surrender of my pride and pretence,
and bless me with humility.
Receive the surrender of my self-will,
and bless me with freedom.
Receive the surrender of my fear and folly,
and bless me with wisdom.

Lord, you are high and holy, and yet you stoop to conquer me, not condemning me for my faults nor making them the barrier to fellowship, but restoring and forgiving me the very moment I believe anew in Jesus my Saviour.
I believe, Lord—and I feel forgiven!

Amen.

II

O you who are the giver of my soul,
forgive me this day for my strange readiness
to become a slave to things temporal.
Forgive those occasional doubts,
those needless anxieties,
those petty interests,
and create in me a greater sensitiveness
to the things that belong to my peace.

I know that you, Lord, offer me pardon
for the greatest and smallest of my faults,
and so I ask your forgiveness
for the times when I was tempted
to suppress the voice of conscience—
and yielded;
for the times when I allowed myself
to think that some good work would save me;
for the times when I conveniently forgot
to give you my wholehearted loyalty.
Grant me, Lord, your pardon and your peace—
and renew a right spirit within me!

Preserve me this day and every day
from the prayer of confession
which forgets about the need for amendment
of life and conduct;
for I know how easy it is to be 'sorry',
and how difficult it is to be 'better'.

O Lord of truth,
replace my hypocrisy by integrity.
O Lord of right,
replace my baseness by sincerity.
O Lord of grace,
replace my apathy by devotion.

Amen.

III

O Lord my God, if I have been
inconsistent or hypocritical in my service of you,
forgive me, I pray.
And hear me as I bring before you
my strange tendency to forget your love for me,
my strange hesitancy to believe in you,
my strange aptitude for *over*-anxiety
and for a too ready submission
to what I mistakenly call my 'fate'.

Lord, I deplore my notable reluctance
to accept the forgiveness I always need.
Lord, I deplore my frequent refusal
to believe in the power of prayer.
Lord, I deplore my obvious tendency
to put self before others,
and to put self before you.

Pardon me, gracious Father,
that I have been easily led away,
that I have 'kept quiet'
when your voice should have been heard,
that I have sat still
when I should have been up and doing.
Sometimes I've even patted myself on the back,
and thought you should do so too!
Lord, if I have blown my own trumpet,
or have practised a thinly disguised altruism,
or have been unduly concerned to 'look good' —
forgive me.
Help me to measure my life
by no lower standard than yours,
and so save myself from distorting pride
and foolish self-satisfaction.

Amen.

IV

Forgive me, O faithful one,
that I knew the right and still did the wrong.
Forgive me, O gracious one,
the pride which made me think I knew best.
Forgive me, O loving one,
that I often disappoint those who love me.

If ever I get into the rut of believing
that the quality of my life is good enough,
stir me, Lord, out of my self-satisfaction,
and may I seek not just 'improvement',
but perfection!
It's certainly easy to recall those times
when I was bitter and unforgiving.
I have remembered old insults and imagined others.
I allowed the sun to go down on my wrath.
Forgive me, O bestower of peace!

Nor can I help deploring, Lord, the self-will
which kept me from consulting you;
the unwillingness to accept advice from others;
the attempts to shout down the voice of conscience.

O ground of all existence,
cast out my faulty reactions to life!
O lover of my soul,
break down my foolish resistance to that love!
O author of freedom,
rebuke my faithless refusal of liberty!

And may the doors of my heart be open now
to receive your forgiveness—and your power.
For Jesus' sake. Amen.

V

Eternal God, though my guilt may be great,
  it is small compared with your glory!
Although my faults may be many,
  your forgiveness swallows them up!
Lord, help me always, frankly and freely,
  to recognise my human frailty,
  but to be even more aware of your power.
Give me courage and honesty and realism
  to see and deplore the worst in myself,
  but save me from failing to see and adore
  the best in you!

I know, Lord, I haven't always treated you fairly,
  even though you have dealt bountifully with me.
I know I haven't always played the game with you,
  even though you have been generous to me.
Prompt me, even now, to a change of heart!
Forgive me that I have sometimes
  become like a frightened rabbit
  running back into the dark burrows
  of watchful alarm;
  that I have sometimes suffered
  a shrinking of soul and collapse of faith
  in face of a sudden crisis or challenge.
And forgive me that I've been so reluctant
  to be different from others.

But now, Lord, I shall not be slow to sing
  'If there is aught of worth in me,
  It comes from thee alone'.
Even in my moments of shame I shall still know
  you are the Father who loves me—and
    forgives me.

Amen.

VI

Sometimes, Lord, I have drawn a veil
  across your glory
  by my unbelief and blindness.
Forgive me, and grant me peace
  and a new vision of you.
Sometimes I have frustrated your purposes
  by my pessimism and lack of persistence.
Forgive me, and grant me a new zeal for you.

I still have to confess, too, Lord,
  that the 'lesser things'
  have not lost all their attraction for me.
I have too readily set a maximum
  for what I'm prepared to do for your cause.
I have frequently succumbed
    to the temptations of the second-best,
    to the temptations of mediocrity,
    to the temptations of 'respectability'.
I have been thankless and insensitive.
I have refused to let you take me
  'out of myself'.
Instead of holding fast the word of life,
  I have sometimes held back from it.

Lord, give me the spirit of adventure
  to replace the spirit of lackadaisicalness.
Lord, give me the spirit of sacrifice
  to replace the spirit of self-seeking.
Lord, give me the spirit of brotherliness
  to replace the spirit of resentment.

    And then how obvious it'll be
    that I am forgiven!

Amen.

VII

O God, I know very well
that your grace is greater than my sin—
but I don't think my sin of no account.
And so I freely confess to you now, Lord,
those things, small or great,
which can only be regarded as failures.
Sometimes I have made unworthy choices;
sometimes I've faltered in the line of duty;
sometimes I've dallied with unwholesome
desires.
Forgive me, O Lord my God!

Great tasks, O God, you want me to do,
but my achievement hasn't always been
great.
You have set me the task of loving—
and I have been so easily irritated.
You have set me the task of witnessing
for you in my daily work—
and I've forgotten that Christianity
is a weekday religion, as well as for
Sundays!

Take from me, O Lord my God,
my pride, my pretence, my prejudice—
and give me a simple humility.
Forgive me that I have sometimes started well
but been a little short on staying power.
Forgive me that I have promised my loyalty
but have sometimes failed to redeem it.
So will you, O forgiving one,
be the strength of my surrendered will;
be the life of my deepest life;
be the voice of my inmost conscience—
and to you I shall give all praise!
Amen.

I

Sometimes, O God, I have prayed with the mind
but not the heart—
save me even now from that error!
Sometimes, O God, I have prayed
and found prayer unreal—
help me to seek the cure in myself!
Sometimes, O God, I have prayed to you
as a grudging instead of a giving God—
forbid that I shall do so now!

Preserve me always, O God,
in the certainty that you do hear
when I call to you,
and that nothing could be more natural
than for me to 'have a word with you'.
O light of my way,
guide me in my prayers and my aspirations.
O Lord of my heart,
lift me up to new devotion and love.
O life of my soul,
grant me to know that I shall be with you.

Grant, too, O Lord,
that I may never pray for those things
which would shame your purpose,
or would insult
the spiritual image of yourself within me.
Lord, I love you; yet help my lovelessness!
Lord, I long for you; yet help my apathy!
Lord, I believe in you; yet help my unbelief!
Amen.

II

Gracious Father, I know that you are
  far readier to listen to me
  than I am to speak to you;
  far readier to speak to me
  than I am to listen to you.
Yet how often have I forgotten it!
Save me from the error
  of calling on you
  as the Unknowable God,
  or as the impersonal power of the universe;
  but let me truly recognise you
  as Father and friend.

O Lord of heaven,
  come down afresh to me on earth!
O Lord of all being,
  fill my soul with your fullness!
O Lord of my heart,
  let your spirit stir me to faith and love!

In these coming days, Father,
  grant that I shall spend less time
  wondering how prayer 'works'
  and more time praying.
Let me acknowledge more openly
  that you are worthy of my worship and
    praise.
Let my communing with you
  always be a lovely and inspiring experience.
Take now the love and longing of my heart
  and draw me nearer to yourself,
  O hearer of the prayers of men!

Amen.

III

You, Lord, are the God of the universe
  and the God who hears prayer!
  Hear mine this day, O Lord!
You, Lord, are truth;
  so may my worship be without pretence.
You, Lord, are life;
  so may my worship be without coldness.
You, Lord, are good;
  so may my worship be without sin.

I know, O God, that you are continually
  calling to us,
  and that you patiently await our call.
Let me remember that my response *could* be
  to wait a little longer in silence,
  rather than to rush into speech.
But, either way, I know you are there,
  and I rejoice in your presence!
You, Lord, have inspired in me
  the desire for a life of purity.
In your strength may I attain it.
You alone, O fountain of life,
  can quench my deepest thirst.
You alone, O bread of life,
  can satisfy my deepest hunger.
    Do so yet again, Lord!

Whenever I make my prayer to you, Lord,
  preserve me from the temptation to 'test' you by
  the 'success' or 'failure' of these prayers!
Let me always be readier to offer thanks for what
  you are than for what you do.
Let these few moments of prayer be lit up with
  something of your glory, so that I may catch a
  gleam of it and bear it with me into the world.
Amen.

IV

O God, your love of me
  is neither sporadic nor limited!
Your favour is for a lifetime!
From life's beginning to its end
  your favour is the air I breathe!
This day, Lord,
  I aspire to be free
  of all that separates me from you.
I desire to commune with you.
I seek to be truly alive for you,
  living with confidence and serenity,
  to the glory of your name.

But sometimes, O Lord my God,
  I have tried to pray to you
  when the channel from my heart to yours
  was blocked by pride.
Sometimes I have invited you
  into an unworthy dwelling-place.
Will you, then, sweep away now
  those things which hinder
  my communion with you, my Father—
  and not least my pride and self-assurance!

Lord, if I have been possessed
  by the spirit of apprehension and fear,
  grant me now the spirit of faith.
Lord, if I have been possessed
  by the spirit of envy or resentment,
  grant me now the spirit of love.
Lord, if I have been possessed
  by the spirit of apathy or heaviness,
  grant me the spirit of hope.

Amen.

V

Lord, you are always waiting for me
  to *want* to 'have a word with you'.
And I know there should be no trouble
  about making the right connections,
  because you are already there, calling me!
There's so much I could talk to you about—
  the vision of wholeness you hold before me;
  the vision of peace;
  the vision of joy;
    and the innumerable concerns of life.
In prayer this day, Lord,
  I open the doors of my heart to the love
  you are continually pouring upon me.
In prayer I acknowledge my need of you
  if I am to achieve my highest aspirations
  and make anything worthwhile of my life.
Without the power which communion with
    you gives,
  I know I would dishonour your name
  and disgrace myself.
Without the deep assurance of your love
  I could have no reason for believing
  in the significance of my life.

Eternal God, you who are my light,
  grant that I may always put behind me
  all those things which darken my soul.
May I more clearly know you
  as the Father who loves me,
  more deeply rejoice in you
  as the Son who has redeemed me, and more
  readily follow you who are the spirit of truth.

Yours, Lord, is the presence
  from which no one can flee.
May I never *want* to!   Amen.

VI

You, Lord, are most readily to be found
  by those whose eyes are always open to you.
May mine be open—
  and may I love what I see!
I know, O God, that I'm utterly dependent
  on your care.
Without your breath I could not breathe.
Without your power I could not move.
Without your love I could not be affectionate.
  I rejoice now in this goodness of yours!

And I rejoice in the comfort of prayer.
Save me from imagining that prayer
  is mainly a matter of asking for things!
Let my prayers be of adoration,
  of thanksgiving, of praise.
Help me to pray for others before myself.
Help me to pray for more power
  rather than for less pain.
Help me to seek you yourself
  before your many blessings.

In a world proclaiming that 'God is dead',
  I proclaim my faith, O gracious one,
  in the Lord who daily bears me up.
Grant that the spirit of prayer and worship
  may prompt my heart daily
  as I bring to you my devotion and praise.
Open my eyes, heavenly Father,
  to see more clearly the needs of others,
  and to realise that my own prayers for self
  are of greatest avail
  when I have also prayed for others.

Through Jesus my Lord.

Amen.

VII

Lord, I'm told to
'call upon you while you are near'.
But it's hard to imagine
that you could ever be far away!
Whenever I have genuinely sought you,
I have found you, Lord.
And again I call on you now,
knowing that you're waiting for my call.
I know, O God, that you want
to have fellowship with me
more than I want to have it with you—
but I really *do* want it now!
Reveal yourself to me afresh, O God!

Eternal God, who are so near to me,
help me more clearly to know you
as the Father who created me;
help me more deeply to rejoice in you
as the Son who redeemed me;
help me more readily to obey you,
the Holy Spirit, as you offer to lead me.

If I have approached you, Lord,
with the aspiration and the hope
of selfish gain,
change me to seek only your will.
If I have ever looked on prayer
as nothing but a method of getting,
help me to adopt it
rather as a method of giving.
If I have ever considered religion a sideline,
may I now see it
as the very stuff of existence.
And grant, O God, that I may believe in you
as a personal God instead of as a vague ideal.
Through the incarnate Jesus. Amen.

I

Lord, I thank you afresh now that you are
not only the maker and sustainer of all things,
but also my redeemer.
For the wonder of the redeeming purpose
which brought my saviour to this earth,
I give you praise, O God.
I rejoice, Lord, that there is
no fickleness about your love for me.
In a world of changing affections and loyalties,
your love is steadfast and deep.
Praise be to you, Lord, for you are
the life of every soul that loves you;
the strength of every mind that seeks you;
the light of every heart that sees you.
Let *me* continue to know you
as life and strength and light!

Lord, for giving me cause to smile
where once I might have frowned;
for giving me cause to hope
where once I might have despaired;
for taking me up into the heights
where once I might have been in the depths—
I thank you, O Lord my God!

And receive the praise of my heart, Lord,
for Him who is the way—the one I've honestly
tried to follow;
for Him who is the truth—the one who has saved
me from embracing a watered-down faith;
for Him who is the life—the one who has brought
a new dimension to my living.
Through the same Jesus my Lord. Amen.

II

There are so many things, Lord,
for which I should thank you:
the cheer and challenge of family life;
the many friendships of the way;
the enrichment of literature, art, science;
the memories of dear ones;
the saving help of Jesus.
Forbid that my thankfulness should ever
have to be 'turned on',
but let it be as natural for me to thank you
as it is for you to love me!

I certainly am thankful to know someone
who will never let me down—
no matter how often I may let Him down.
I certainly am thankful to know
that my saviour can be depended upon
for forgiveness and support.
How wonderful to live in the atmosphere
of your eternal faithfulness!
How wonderful to know that I can
'have a word with God'!

And now I gratefully acknowledge, O God,
that without your gracious will
I could not even breathe.
It is your wonderful providence
which sustains me in life and in joy.
You have given me freedom of will
by which to choose for or against you—
and I thank you for helping me
to make the really sensible choice!

Amen.

III

There is nothing dearer to me, O God,
than the consciousness of your presence.
Without it, my life is just jogging along,
my song is in low key—indeed, off key!
But you *are* dwelling in me, Lord,
and I feel a new being.
So praise be yours!

Today, Lord, I'm full of thanksgiving
in that you've continually had faith in me,
even though I have often let you down;
in that you've continually hoped
(almost against hope, it would seem!)
I would rouse myself from my mediocre living
and set my sights on high;
in that you have continued to love me
despite my many wanderings and weaknesses.

Many of us, Lord, take life's blessings
with no thought of the love prompting them.
Some even think the world owes them a living!
And if some are thankful at all, Lord,
it's a kind of grudging appreciation.
But as for me this day, O God,
I will give thanks to you
with my whole heart!
My very life comes from you, Lord.
To you I owe my present comforts.
To you I owe my hope of life eternal.
What great cause have I, then,
to 'praise the Lord, his mercies trace,
praise his providence and grace'!

Amen.

IV

You have blessed me greatly, Lord,
in the days that lie behind me—
but sometimes I have forgotten
you have so much to do with it.
Forgive me, Father, and give me
the blessing of a thankful heart
even as I pray now.
For the courage you give me
to face life, I thank you, Lord.
For the confidence you give me
to transform my cares, I thank you, Lord.
For the compassion you give me
to ennoble my soul, I thank you, Lord.

How I rejoice today
that you continually offer me the power
by which to make myself a new creation.
How I rejoice that you draw near to me
in every good thought that I think
and in every good deed that I do.
How I rejoice that you have a loving purpose
not simply for the world as a whole,
but for me as an individual!
Praise and thanks be yours, O God.

Thanks be yours, O Saviour Christ,
for forgiving me my faults.
Thanks be yours, O Saviour Christ,
for fortifying me in temptation.
Thanks be yours, O Saviour Christ,
for fashioning me in your likeness.
Now be with me in the problems I must face,
in the friendships I shall enjoy,
in the dreams I shall dream—
and in all things may I give you the praise.
Amen.

V

For the divine provision sustaining me
  I thank you, O God.
For the divine presence lighting up my life
  I thank you, O God.
For the divine promise bringing me hope
  I thank you, O God.

And how fervently, Lord, I praise you today
  that you have blessed me with life
  and brought me joyfully to this hour;
  that you have blessed me with light
  and shown me the pathway to tread;
  that you have blessed me with love
  and shown me the meaning of fellowship.
Thank you, Father of all,
  for the love my friends have shown me;
  for the knowledge others are praying for me;
  for the measure of wellbeing which I enjoy;
  for the peace I found amid perplexity.
Yet help me more and more to rejoice in you
  as the deepest reality of my life.

O doer of good, I thank you
  for the nobility of ordinary labour.
O lover of men, I thank you
  for the sacredness of human personality.
O creator of life, I thank you
  for the hope of life eternal.
Let me never cease to praise you
  that, though you are the eternal God,
  you became man, and lived on this earth,
  to show me what you are really like.
Through the same Jesus, my Saviour.
Amen.

VI

Your creative presence is ever around me, Lord;
 let me 'feel' it, and then let me live
 a truly creative life for you.
Your blessings are more than I can number;
 but let me know at least some of them
 for what they really are—tokens of your love.
In reverence and in thanksgiving, O Christ,
 I bow before your Cross
 and magnify you for the love
 which prompted your self-sacrifice.
You are the giver of every good gift,
 and you have given me
 even the gift of a thankful heart
 by which to *value* all your gifts.
Accept the praise of my heart, Lord,
 as I thank you now
  for the life which is stirring within me;
  for the light which is shining upon me;
  for the love which is smiling upon me.

And I thank you afresh, Saviour Christ,
 that you have taken hold of me;
 that you are holding on to me;
 that you will never let me go.
May I constantly seek
 to place myself within the sphere
 of your redemptive power;
 and when I feel it, may I rejoice
 and desire that others feel it too.

And receive my thanks, Lord, for those
 with whom the hours pass only too quickly;
 who have known me at my worst
  and still love me;
 whose lives have helped me
  to get into touch with you. Amen.

VII

Today, Lord, I would thank you
  for the way in which you have brought me
    through my troubles and problems;
  for the peace and assurance
    which I have found in you;
  for the strength and hope
    which have come as I communed with you.
And I give you thanks
  for my family and my friends;
  for those who will continue to trust me;
  for the interests and comforts of life;
  for those who will continue to believe in me;
  for the joy of 'having a word with you';
  for those who will insist
    on judging me generously.

In that you are the light that lights
  every man who comes into the world,
    I thank you, O God.
In that you are the love that surrounds
  every man who comes into the world,
    I thank you, O God.
In that you are the life that surges
  through every man who comes into the world,
    I thank you, O God.

How I rejoice, O God,
  that you can inject my experience of life
    with the salt of good humour,
  and relieve the solemnity of living
    with the gift of wholesome laughter.
Thank you, O fountain of life,
  for all that keeps my life balanced and sane,
  for bringing light into my eyes
    and warmth into my heart,
  for the ability to see a joke. Amen.

THE DIVINE DELIVERER

I

O you who save the crushed in spirit,
  I remember that you have been the deliverer
  of your people throughout every age.
Receive my praise now, Lord,
  that when my own spirit was crushed,
  you revived and strengthened me!
For the courage you have given me
  to face life, I thank you, Lord.
For the confidence you have given me
  to transform my cares, I thank you, Lord.
For the strength you have given me
  to cope with my problems, I thank you, Lord.

So often, Lord, you've brought me
  out of darkness and despair—
  and yet I *still* wander off into the darkness
  and into the shadows of despair.
And sometimes so needlessly!
And so, Lord, while I know you can deliver me,
  help me *not* to despair
  when things don't seem to go smoothly.
Let me accept each day your invitation
  to come with you,
  so that I may build up a relationship of trust,
  and be empowered for the challenges of life.

Now be with me, Lord, in the problems I
    must face,
  making me joyful in the divine provision
  which sustains me,
  and in the divine promise which brings me hope.
And if I am in danger of letting go of you, or of
  letting you down, never let me go, or let me down,
  O great deliverer!   Amen.

II

O comforter of my soul, I approach you today
with praise on my lips,
for you have made my heart joyful
at the remembrance of your goodness to me.
Even in the midst of pain
I have found your peace.
Even in the midst of perplexity
I have found assurance.
Even in the midst of peril
I have found strength.

I rejoice too, Lord, that you have so often
delivered me from myself—
that you have assured me
it's worth having another try—
that you have released me
from the dungeon of hopelessness.

And because I know you as *my* deliverer, Lord,
I pray you to be the deliverer of others.
O you whose will is that men be whole,
deliver them from sickness and suffering.
O you who offer redemption to everyone,
deliver men from their doubts and disbelief
and bring them the joy of your salvation.

Eternal God, who can radically transform life for us,
I acknowledge again that you have so often
'brought me out into an open place';
now deliver me from my faults,
from my worries,
from my weakness.
And let me go out to praise you,
my deliverer and my delight! Amen.

III

You, Lord, have made me, and won me;
  and you have brought me to this hour.
Grant that I may never lose the feeling
  that you are my divine king,
  that you are my greatest hope,
  that you are my strong deliverer.
Will you do with me always
  what will best serve the purpose of good—
  and I shall rejoice so to be used.
Deliver me from my lack of compassion,
  and make me more loving and more 'feeling'
  as I live in your world.
Deliver me from my preoccupation with number
    one,
  and give me grace to love and serve my
    neighbours.
Deliver me from my intolerance of others,
  and let me show tolerance and consideration
  to those I don't find it easy to like.

You alone, O God, can bring me out of myself
  and help me look outwards rather than inwards.
You can help me face disappointment and
    tragedy.
You can prompt me through your word
  to believe that I can do all things
  through Christ who strengthens me.
    Do this for me now, O Lord!
Redeem and strengthen the life I live
  so that the love of my heart,
          the thought of my mind,
          the works of my hands
  may be a worthwhile offering to you,
  and I shall feel it a life well lived.
          Through Christ my Saviour.   Amen.

IV

Where I am weak, O Lord,
  will you bring forth strength.
Where there is darkness, Lord,
  will you bring forth light.
Where I am unfeeling, Lord,
  will you bring forth love.

I remember today, O Lord,
  that you haven't offered to be the cushion,
  but the stronghold of my life!
So let me be readier to seek you
  as deliverer than as refuge;
  readier to be transformed
  than to be pandered to.
Let me live always in the light,
  with a buoyant heart
  and strong in your great strength.
May my good intentions have your approval,
  and may my misguided ideas receive
  both your rebuke and your redirection.
Deliver me, O God,
  from anything that is unworthy
  in my attitude to life,
  or in my thoughts and deeds.

Let nothing disturb my soul, O redeemer—
  and may it be fixed on you.
Let nothing drag my soul down, O sustainer—
  and may it be held up by you.
Let nothing turn my soul aside, O deliverer—
  and may it be guided by you.

Amen.

V

You, Lord, are the life of my life,
  and the strength of my life;
  and I rejoice today that you
  have often caused me to have hope
  when I might well have been in despair;
  that you have taken me up into the heights
  when I might well have been down in the
    depths.
I thank you, Lord, that you have had
  at least some success in prompting me
  to seek a right attitude towards life
  rather than a life made easy for me.
You have delivered me from the temptation
  to fritter life away
  on unworthy projects or pleasures.
Continue this work in me, O God!

Lord, if your reign over men's hearts
  is to be extended in our world,
  some of us will have to be delivered
  from our hesitancy, or timidity, our 'mildness'!
Give *me* strength to witness more forcefully.
Give me courage to face all that is
  inimical to your sacred cause.
Deliver me from the subtle desire
  to see things kept as they are.
Grant me that brand of courage
  which dares any consequence of being true to you;
  which will gladly attempt the impossible;
  which is willing to be laughed at.

Make me, O God, far readier to seek your face
  than to seek my fortune,
  far readier to ask for your deliverance
  than to side-step your claim.
    For my Saviour's sake.   Amen.

VI

How often, Lord, I've felt inadequate
  for the demands of life!
How often I've been in despair—
    my courage sapped;
    my resolves frustrated;
    my faith weakened.
But thank you for the transformation
  which took place when I felt your spirit
  surging into me!
You have raised me to life and liberty,
  O Lord and deliverer.
You have given me a new urge to live for you.
You have helped me to remember
  that resurrection follows the cross.

If in days ahead clouds hang over me,
  chase them away, O spirit of light.
If I find myself listless and unconcerned
  about your will for me,
  bring me a new dynamic, O spirit of life.
If I show myself resentful and unloving,
  give me gentleness and charity, O spirit of
    love.

O divine deliverer, grant strength and courage
  to those who must make important decisions;
  to those sorely tempted to do wrong;
  to those obsessed by the idea
    that life is too much for them.

You know, Lord, the duties that now lie before me;
  give me zeal by which to do them.
You know, Lord, the hazards I'll have to face;
  give me courage in which to face them.
You know, Lord, the sins I'm prone to;
  give me strength by which to conquer them.
Amen.

VII

You, Lord, are a solid foundation for my life!
You, Lord, are the redeemer of my soul!
  Praise be to you, O my deliverer.
You have given me your incarnate self
  that I may have a centre and a saviour.
May he be the pattern of my life now
  and the promise of what it will be.

But I'm well aware there is still darkness in me
  needing to be chased away by your light.
There is still weakness in me
  needing to be transformed by your strength.
There is still a sense of frustration
  needing to be driven away by your love.
Sometimes, Lord, I have thought I was
    'finished'—
  but you knew I had hardly begun!
Sometimes I thought I was a 'dead loss'—
  but you knew what life, and what profit,
  there was still to be brought out in me!
Thank you for doing it, O God!

Deliver me, O gracious one,
  from a greater interest in existing
    than in living;
  from preferring to 'play safe' with life
    than 'taking a chance' with you;
  from being more anxious to help myself
    than to help others.
Help me, O Lord, in the midst of strain and
    stress,
  to remember your purposes will be achieved.
Help me, O Lord, in the midst of suffering,
  to remember the victory of the Cross.
And to you, my God and my deliverer,
  I shall give the praise and the glory! Amen.

I

O Lord of all being,
before whom I bow at this time
and to whom I commit myself anew,
grant that I may see you clearly
as the One who has a claim on me.
You, Lord, want me;
yet how reluctant I am to enlist!
O you who are the way,
may I more successfully walk in it.
O you who are the truth,
may I more completely acknowledge it.
O you who are the life,
may I more effectively absorb it.

Let my earnest desire, O God,
be to possess the mind of Christ—
and give me perseverance
as I seek my goal.
Let me be fully aware that dedication
to my Saviour is not 'once and for all',
but that each day brings the call
to re-dedication and commitment.
And so, Father, into your hands
I commit myself this day, asking that you will
infuse into me a new humility;
bestow on me a new understanding;
form within me a new heart.

But grant too that I shall not
be held back or reduced to despair
at my past failures in love and life.
Give me diligence to seek you, Lord!
Give me patience to see you, Lord!
Give me understanding to serve you, Lord! Amen.

II

O God, you who desire
that I risk my all in an act
of loving commitment to your Son,
if I have been too self-centred,
or been too keen to be 'safe',
forgive me, I pray.
May I remember you've made me
so that I can respond
to everything that is good and true—
especially the good and the truth
which you are.
So help me, Lord, to put you
in the centre of my thinking and doing.
May I acknowledge you afresh
as my divine king,
as my greatest hope,
as my strong deliverer.
And give yourself to me, Lord,
as again I give myself to you.

O you who prompt my deepest longings,
bless me with these now!
O you who inspire my truest love,
bless me with it now!
O you who sustain my richest life,
bless me with it now!

I come to you, O my Saviour,
asking that I may never
say one thing and do another.
So grant that I shall never do
anything to invalidate my own claim
to be your committed servant.
For your own name's sake.
Amen.

III

Today, Lord, I ask you to make me
  more willing to 'take a chance' with you
  than to 'play safe' with life.
Let me welcome you afresh into my life.
Grant that love of self may perish
  as a moth in the flame,
  and that your gift, already in me,
  may be vigorously stirred up.
In my worship and in my seeking
  may I have singleness of purpose,
  and may I never succumb to the temptation
  of wanting the best of two worlds—
    but may love and serve only you.

Many things, Lord, I may rightly seek,
  but your kingdom is first on my list!
Thanks be yours, O Christ,
  that you have inspired me
  to get my priorities straight!
And as I bring myself to you again,
  I pray that what is good in me
  may prevail over what is evil.
By me, Lord, let your name be hallowed!
In me, Lord, let your kingdom come!

O you who call to every man,
  may I have no regrets or reservations
  that I have accepted the holy calling
  of a life dedicated to you, my Lord.
O you who seek to possess me,
  help me to want to be possessed.
And I rejoice again, O gracious Lord,
  that despite all my undeserving,
  your love will not let me go.

Amen.

IV

O you who are king of my heart,
  how willing a subject I am!
Be in my mind, O Lord,
  so that no impure thought may invade it.
Be in my heart, O Lord,
  so that no lovelessness may desecrate it.
Be in my hands, O Lord,
  so that no unclean thing may be done by them.
Set me apart for yourself, O God,
  and give to me the quiet mind
    and the loving heart
  with which to live in joy and peace.
Grant that I may bring to you now,
  in renewed affection and dedication,
    the gold of obedience,
    the incense of lowliness,
    the tenderness of love.

I know, Lord, that I shall not be equipped
  to do your work in this community
  unless I am fully committed to you.
Confirm me now in this commitment.
Let me know more what it means
  to be crucified with Christ,
    and to rise again with him.
Your love and your strength, O Lord,
  should inspire me to do my best,
  and to be at my best.
So may I do, and so may I be!

I know, Lord, I've often felt
  a warm glow of love for you—
  and then found my love growing cold.
Forbid, Lord, that this shall happen again!
    For your own name's sake.   Amen.

V

Sometimes, O God, I am only too ready
  to 'get by' in my daily living
  without showing what I'm made of—
  or what *you* can make me.
Now let me welcome any challenges
  to my faith,
  and in your power may I come out on top!
I know very well, Lord, I'm not exhorted
  to follow your path leisurely
  but to commit my way to you.
Let me do this—now.
Let me remember that a cross,
  not a cushion,
  is the symbol of the Faith.
Let me more clearly know you
  as the Father who dearly loves me,
  more deeply rejoice in you
  as the Son who has redeemed me,
  more readily follow you
  who are the spirit of truth.

O you who are the New Man
  who can work the miracle of faith in me,
  I praise you that you are able to do for me
  what I cannot possibly do for myself.
Give me no greater desire in life
  than to be among your children,
  and to be utterly dedicated to you—
  and in this sacred experience, Lord,
  may I find my life and my peace.

Bless me, O Lord my God,
  with a real sense of your indwelling,
  and may the sweetness of this moment
  remain with me until I lie down to sleep.
Amen.

VI

I keep the Lord always before me,
 says the Psalmist — but sometimes I've tried
 to keep you well behind me, Lord —
 as far behind as possible!
Sometimes I have set you aside altogether.
Forgive me, and help me
 to reach out to a new commitment.
I know that I have stood at the crossroads
 and not known which road to take.
I know that I have hesitated
 and declined the directions you offered.
Show me the path of life, O God,
 and may I with confidence and with
  dedication
 walk along it.

O goal of men's souls,
 make me more and more sensitive
 to the call and promise of heaven.
O truth of men's minds,
 make me more and more able
 to understand the deep things of the Faith.
O light of men's bodies,
 make me more and more responsive
 to the liberating power of your spirit.

O Christ my Lord,
 you have given me your incarnate self
 so that I might have a centre and saviour.
Be the pattern of my life now
 as I commit myself utterly to you.
May I be drawn out of myself,
 and drawn up to you!
For your own name's sake.
Amen.

VII

O you who in Christ Jesus
have shown me what real loyalty is,
I pray today that I may be true to myself
and true to you, my Lord.
If my love for you has grown cold,
and I've been casual and uncommitted,
help me rekindle the flame of love
and restore my urge to be wholly yours.
Grant that today and every day I may answer
your call to commitment;
your call to communion;
your call to compassion.

Sometimes, Father, I seem more interested
to 'put on airs' than to 'put on Christ'.
And even more shamefully—
to put up with him
rather than to put him on!
But, albeit dimly, I feel that it's
only by losing myself in you
that I shall really find my true self.

Renew within me, O God,
a realisation of my high calling;
a realisation of my hidden capacities;
a realisation of your holy cause.
May I know more and more
that your hand is laid upon me for good;
that your purpose of good for me
is not a figment of my imagination;
that your promise of good awaits only
my receptive and dedicated heart
for its fulfilment.

Amen.

LOVE FOR OTHERS

I

Your directions, Lord, are quite clear—
  that we should love one another.
Tolerating one another isn't enough, Lord!
  But I know it's very common—and so is
    snobbery, paternalism, condescension.
We put up with people.
We put in time with people.
  But how often do we love them, Lord?
Shouldn't *I* be far more aware that
    'All are brethren far and wide,
    Since thou, O Lord, for *all* hast died'?

Let me, Lord, be more anxious
  to offer my friendship to others—
  remembering what a friend *I* have in Jesus!
Let me find a deeper love for others—
  remembering how deeply you continue to love me.
I know, Lord, that my love is lukewarm,
  when it should abound for you.
So give me greater wisdom, O God,
  to see where love is really needed;
  and give me a stronger urge
  to make more than a token contribution!
Lead me, heavenly Father,
  through all the changes and chances of life
  in an unchangeable love for you and for others.

In all my dealings with others
  may I have a real largeness of heart,
  rejoicing with others in their joy,
  and sorrowing with them in their grief.
Now and always, Lord, may I
  think in love, pray in love, walk in love—
  for your glory. Amen.

II

I know, Lord, that the Apostle
 was echoing his master in telling us
 to let love be genuine.
But the love that dissimulates
 is so easy to find around me!
Some shamefully use others in the name of
 'love'.
Some are just tolerated
 when they think they're being loved.
Preserve me, Lord, from this travesty of love!

O God of love, in acknowledging those ties
 which bind me closely to dear ones,
 I pray you to break down those barriers
 which divide me from those
 who could—or should—be my friends.
Lord, may *my* love be without dissimulation!
May I be less hypocritical
 in my relationships with other people;
 less condescending; less cynical.
Let me remember the love which lies
 at the heart of all things.

Preserve me, Lord, from thinking
 that I fulfil my Christian responsibilities
 to others by praying for them,
 when there is some practical action I could
 take to help them.
Let me be more alive to the possibility
 of taking such action,
 and forbid that, today, I shall leave undone
 some good that I could do for others.
 For Jesus' sake.
 Amen.

III

No one, O Christ, can fully understand the
mystery
of the Father's love for you—
or, indeed, of your love for me!
But in faith I affirm my conviction
of the eternal nature of love,
and of your embodiment of it.
Otherwise, why are you so patient and tolerant
towards me when I am unloving?
Those uncharitable feelings towards others,
for instance.
Those side-steppings of Christian responsibility.

Of course, Lord, I ask you to bless
those who feel unloved or are lonely—
but maybe your blessing could come most
quickly
to a few people,
if *I* loved or befriended them!
Of course I ask you to bless the refugees—
but maybe that blessing would be clearer
if I sent some hard cash!

Give me grace, Lord, to efface self
and to disown all 'aggressiveness'
in my attitude towards others.
Take me more and more 'out of myself',
so that I may *enjoy* Christian service
and be a real ambassador for Christ.
Let the fire of your love, O Christ,
purge and possess my soul,
and in my daily life, O lover of all,
may I not only feel but radiate
some of that warmth which your love brings.
Amen.

IV

I rejoice, O Christ my saviour, that
  'in love, from love, thou camest forth'.
May I be rooted and grounded
  in that same eternal and ever-present love!
May I absorb more and more of it
  so that my whole life will be suffused
  with its fragrance.

I know you want to use me daily in your
    purpose
  of redeeming the world.
Grant then that men may see in my face
  the reflection—however dim—of him
  who is the way, the truth, the life.
In all my relationships with others
  may I put away all jealousy
  and be made more generous in spirit;
  may I put away my easy resentments
  and be made more forgiving.

Let me, Lord, be far readier to pray in love
  for those countless ones who need you:
  those who feel grossly inadequate for life;
  those who feel they're making
    little or no progress on their pilgrim way;
  those who imagine they are too sinful
    ever to be forgiven.
Reveal yourself in your love and power, Lord,
  and if there's any way in which you can use
    me,
  here I am, Lord!
For your love's sake I pray.
Amen.

V

I live, O God, in a world
full of suspicion and torn by dissension—a world
in which 'brotherliness' is at a premium.
And so I ask you, my Elder Brother,
who are not ashamed to call us brothers,
that men should speedily find a deeper
understanding of one another, and make a real
venture of faith *in* one another.
Grant that *I* at least will be prepared today
to understand and to love others;
and even if I am disappointed with their
response,
may I still be prepared to forgive,
and to try again.

Remove, O God, my foolish prejudices
and those unnecessary provocations
which sometimes arise between me and others.
May I myself be free from the self-will
that must have its own way.
May I never demand standards from others
that I myself am not prepared to adopt.
May I never regard the 'service of others'
as just a pious phrase or a fringe duty.
And so when I hear the song
'O brother man, fold to thy heart thy brother,'
may I join in—as one who has done so!

May your blessing, O Lord, rest on
the self-centred, and may they learn
kindliness—perhaps through me;
the 'hard-boiled', and may they soften
in your warmth;
those who are bitter, and may they learn
to love and forgive.
For Jesus' sake. Amen.

VI

Eternal God, you have asked me to love others
whether I *like* them or not.
I know it's not easy, Lord.
Maybe others feel this way about me!
But give me the grace to obey your
commandment.
When others irritate me, let me remember
how often I might have been condemned
for irritating you, O God.
When others act selfishly
with no regard for my feelings,
help me to remember how you have
forgiven
my selfishness and self-regard.

Lord Jesus, save me
from the bitterness which makes me
cherish grudges against people;
from the unforgiving spirit which so sadly
keeps me apart from my fellowmen.
Let me acknowledge, O God of love, that
'to worship rightly is to love each other,
each smile a hymn, each kindly deed a
prayer'.

In the life of each day, O Lord,
may I demonstrate that love towards others
which seeks no return
but which inevitably gets it;
that love which seeks no reward other than
that of being able to love others more.

You, O God, love me. May I love you!
You, O God, love all people. May I love them
too!

Amen.

VII

I know, O Lord my God,
  that yours is an unchanging love,
  higher than the heights above.
Grant that in response to that love
  I may manifest a new faith and a new fervour.

Save me, Lord, from that unhealthy loneliness
  which often leads to a false sense of values,
  and from that insular attitude to life
  which makes me blind or indifferent
  to the very existence of others.
Let your love for all men
  be a marvel—and a joy—to me.
Let me more deeply realise that, without it,
  my own life would be like a ready-laid fire
  lacking the vital spark to kindle it into flame.
May the warmth of your love, Lord,
  thaw my frequent coldness towards people.
If I have been too self-centred
  or too keen to be 'safe',
  or have dishonoured the full manhood
  which lies within my power to express,
    forgive me, O God.
Let my whole life be a ministry of good.
May I be more interested in helping than
    having.
May I always regard it as a privilege
  to be your ambassador, O Lord.
May your light shine so brightly in me
  that I myself may become a lamp
  to all those who meet me.
And grant that your matchless love
  shall possess me so completely
  that I may find it as 'natural' to love others
  as to love myself!   Amen.

I

O God, you've made it possible for me
to achieve 'stature' through Christ.
Grant that my goal and my achievement
may never be too far apart!
Lord, give me the integrity and faith to do what lies at my hands with a real sense of mission.
As I go about the business of life, may my heart throb with that concern which expresses itself not only in prayer but also in dynamic witness.

Forbid that I shall frustrate your purpose through ignorance or thoughtlessness, but school me in the things I should know and the things I should do.
Let me continually reflect that light
which is seen to perfection in Jesus.
Wean me from the temptation to think that I can witness to you only by doing extraordinary things—but help me to find joy and satisfaction doing ordinary things in an extraordinary way!
Grant me increasingly the desire, Lord,
to be healed of every unworthy emotion,
of every ungenerous motive,
of every ignorant thought,
so that I may be a more effective channel
of your blessing to others.

And in the life of discipleship
which you give me to live,
may no task be too hard for me to do;
may no challenge be too great for me to face;
may no suffering be too grievous for me to bear.
For Jesus' sake. Amen.

II

You, Lord, have called me into your
    kingdom,
  and I have taken your call seriously—
  even though I've still a long way to go!
Continue to be my companion on the way.
Forbid that I should ever be satisfied
  with having made a good start,
  but give me the grace to finish with zeal.
Sometimes, Lord, we become disciples
  and have little intention
  of developing our spiritual muscles!
Sometimes, Lord, we become 'babes in Christ'
  and have little intention
  of building ourselves up on spiritual food!
Forbid that I should ever do this, O God!

In every call of Christian duty,
  and in every opportunity of service,
  I know there's the touch of your grace.
And how glad I am that I have found blessing
  whenever I did answer such calls!
But some calls I have not answered.
I resisted your rule over me,
  and so I frustrated my witness for you.
Forgive me, O God.

Now may my discipleship be more real
  than ever before.
Give me greater courage to witness,
  despite the hostility—or apathy—around
    me.
Let me find a real sense of being
  a co-worker in the divine project
  of filling men's hearts with love for you!
Amen.

III

You have placed your image within me, Lord.
Let me daily accept the challenge this entails,
so that the 'common round' may be redeemed
from triviality.
Give me grace to live for the things
that really matter—for the *One* who matters!
Your name has only begun to be glorified
in me, Lord;
but I thank you for the hope and the
promise of better things.
Give me, Lord, the courage
to stand firmly against all forms of evil
as I meet them in the world—
cruelty, hatred, intolerance, injustice.
May I always be ready to serve the cause of peace,
remembering how blessed are the peacemakers.

Some Christians, Lord, seem a bit self-conscious.
Some flourish all right in church,
where the opposition is light.
But when it comes to the crunch, Lord,
they're unwilling to show their true colours.
Lord, let me know nothing of this timidity—
nothing of this shame-faced paralysis!
Let my song be loud and clear:
'I'm not ashamed to own my Lord,
Or to defend his cause'.
May I always have that gladness
and that dynamism
which makes people conscious of my having
something really worth having.
For Jesus' sake. Amen.

IV

O God, how easily I am sometimes swayed
from my intention to follow my master;
and how impatient I become
with the movement of your hand
among this world's events.
I want you to do things my way.
I am loth to move in the proper rhythm
of your purpose,
and to wait on your will.
Forgive me, I pray.

All my powers of body, mind, and spirit
are yours, O Lord.
Sanctify them for your work and witness.
Let me always be more anxious
to have the right attitude towards life
than to have life made easy for me.
Let me be readier to help you, Lord,
than to be helped by you—
though I'll never refuse your help!
Let me remember your approval is based
not so much on the amount I've done for
you,
but on the spirit of the task.

Now let me know even more clearly
the way in which I should go.
Make me proud to be a disciple of yours,
and never 'apologise' for my faith.
May I be more sensitive to the part
I can play in helping your kingdom come,
and give me fullness of joy in playing it.
Amen.

V

I rejoice this day, Lord,
in the transforming truth which has
enriched my Christian experience.
You have made me understand my sacred duty
to pass on something of this truth to others.
But in all my witness to you, Lord,
grant that I may act not because of the reward
I may get, but because I can do no other—for
my soul simply exults in you,
My God and my Saviour!
You have raised me to life and liberty, Lord.
You have made me a new creation—
someone with the capacity to do great things
for you and your cause.
Help me to do them!

Lord, you need people with a sense of mission;
not just evangelists, but social workers, workers
among refugees and the underprivileged, rescue
teams, youth leaders, and the rest.
Give your world, Lord, such people—
people with a social conscience,
people with an urge to lose themselves
in your service.
And let *me* be directed as you think best.
Give me a vision of what I may do for you
in my community,
in my church,
in my home.

I know, Lord, that I'm justified by faith.
I know that my faith in you brings
joy to your own heart.
But I know too that faith without works is dead.
May *my* faith, then, be very much alive—now and
always. Amen.

VI

Often we have made promises, Lord,
and not fulfilled them.
Often we have sworn to be loyal disciples,
but have let you down.
May I, O God, renew my vows now—
and give me strength to perform them!
Let others know me
not only by the faith I profess,
but by the fruits I produce.
Save me, Lord, from the temptation
of 'hiding behind' my Christian profession.
Let me always be aware
that deeds speak louder than words.
May I think larger thoughts and do nobler deeds,
not hesitating but hastening to do your will as
I see it.
May Christian duty not be a drudgery,
but a delight, O Lord!

O you who reconciled the world to yourself
in Christ Jesus, my Lord,
continue his work in me,
that I may be his fragrance among men.
Save me from ever thinking that
because I am 'converted', there is no need
for me to get right with you daily.
So help me to regard my conversion not as the end
but the beginning of my great pilgrimage—and
let me do great things for you as I walk along
the road!

O Lord, I pray you then
to take from my lips every evil word;
to take from my mind every evil thought;
to take from my hands every evil deed—
for your name's sake. Amen.

VII

Today, Lord, I pray
  that my life may be more worthy of you,
  but that I may *never* be completely satisfied
  with the quality of my discipleship.
May I never lapse into an attempt
  to 'bribe' you with my prayers, Lord—
  promising to 'go through the motions'
  if you'll make things easier for me.
Put your strength into my mind,
  so that I may choose bravely
    and bravely stand by my decisions.
Put your love into my heart,
  so that I may know Christ dwells there.
Put your truth into my mouth, so that I may
  speak of him who is the great hope of the world.

May my life, Lord, really shine for you
  like a light in a dark place.
May I have the grace to do good works,
  and when men see them,
  may they glorify you, O God.
Save me from the sin of 'keeping quiet'
  when your voice should have been heard.
Save me from the sin of sitting still
  when I should be 'up and doing'.
Let me rejoice continually
  in the pattern of life I see in Jesus;
  in the portion of life I have from him;
  in the power for living he has injected into me.

May I have the eye which is quick
  to see things I can do for you.
May I have the heart which is quick
  to turn towards others in love.
May I have the mind which is quick
  to think up lovely things to do.   Amen.

INTERCESSION

I

O Father of all, I know it's your will
  that I pray for others as well as myself.
Hear me now, Lord, as I pray
  for those who are of service to me;
  for those whom I serve;
  for those who perform important tasks;
  for those who carry heavy responsibilities;
  for those who are sick and sad.

Bless all those who do good
  and those who try to serve you
  with a good conscience.
And I remember today that there are many
  for whom the coming hours will be
  but a succession of trials and cares;
  and so, Lord, I pray for those
    who are going through the valley of the
      shadow;
    who are held captive by infirmity;
    who are losing hope.
Bless them as you have blessed me.

Be with all those, O God,
  who think noble thoughts and do heroic deeds
  and may those who have the strength to
    persevere
  know the delight of victory.
Let none of your followers, Lord,
  be held back or reduced to despair
  at past failures in love and life—
  but let them all walk forward
  in the liberty and the light
  of your presence.
      For Jesus' sake.   Amen.

II

This day, O God of love,
  I pray for those towards whom
  I am especially drawn in compassion.
May none of them love their lives so much
  that they lose them—and lose you!
Knowing that you are their life,
  may they not be weary.
Knowing that you are their hope,
  may they not despair.
Knowing that you are their shepherd,
  may they not want.

I know, gracious Lord, there are millions
  whose needs are greater than I can number.
I bring them before you now, in prayer:
  the poor and the downcast;
  the weak and the helpless;
  the sick and the refugee.
Minister to their needs, O God,
  and give them a fresh vision of your love
  and a deeper experience of your power.
Bless those who have been pronounced incurable;
Bless those from whom all hope seems to have gone;
Bless those who have been shattered by misfortune—
  and give them to know that they still have
  entrance into your kingdom of life and love.

I pray for those who claim to be atheists;
    for those who love to scorn religion;
    for those who seem insensitive to you.
May your word, Lord, stir them
  into life and love.

Amen.

III

Today, O gracious Father, I would pray
for the lonely and the self-pitying,
that they may feel your love for them;
for the fearful and fretting,
that they may find your peace;
for the sick and the sorrowing,
that they may find the wholeness they seek.

Grant to your people, O God,
that they may not fear any loss,
since you can more than make it good;
that they may not fear any disappointment,
since you can transform tragedy into
triumph;
that they may not fear any challenge,
since they can do all things through Christ.
Let men's souls be flooded with that peace
which the world cannot give, or take away,
and grant that men and women may find
the spirit of anticipation
as they face life with you.

I know, Lord, that I'm far from perfect,
but I remember before you now
those who seem to be insensitive to your word;
those who spurn your invitation to pilgrimage;
those who seem satisfied with a standard
of mere decency.
Confront them, O God!
O you who are the author of faith,
grant fresh hope to the despairing.
O you who are the saviour of men,
grant breadth of soul
to those whose vision is dim.
For your name's sake.

Amen.

IV

O source of healing power,
  let men turn to you for strength!
O source of liberating joy,
  let men turn to you for buoyancy of spirit!
O source of hallowed peace,
  let men turn to you for serenity of mind!
    And so may I!

I pray, Lord, for all those
  who are treading the way of the Cross,
  and have sacrificed much for you.
Bless those who preach your passion and
    power
  in the distant places of the earth.
Strengthen those who witness for you at home.
May all of us do what we know
  of your holy and perfect will;
  and so may we know your peace.
Bless those with high ideals,
  and grant them to be carried out.
Bless those who put duty before pleasure
  and those who overcome many temptations.

O Lord of life and love,
  turn your people's sorrows into song;
  turn your people's cares into trust;
  turn your people's frustrations
    into a means of grace.
Send light to any who may this day
  be groping in darkness.
Send hope to those who despair.
Send peace to those
  who are frantic with anxiety.
For Jesus' sake.

Amen.

V

With the consciousness of your care of me
I come to you now, Lord,
with the needs of others on my heart.
Bless those who suffer grievous pain,
and are grievously handicapped by
weakness.
Bless those whose recovery is so long delayed
that they are growing impatient,
and are becoming depressed.
Bless those who have heavy burdens to carry
and difficult things to do.
Give them your conquering strength, Lord!

O word of God, restore those
whose ears have been deaf to your voice.
O Son of God, restore those
whose eyes are blind to your nature.
O spirit of God, restore those
whose wills are resisting your power.

Hear my prayer, O Lord,
for those who lack strength and courage,
that they may discover the
limitless resources of your strength;
for those whose minds are charmed by evil,
that your power may break the spell;
for those whose souls are in danger,
that they may find life more abundant.

Your mercy is greater than men's sin, Lord;
and so may all your people realise
that you will bless those who try hard
as well as those who cry hard!

Amen.

VI

O God, the Lord and redeemer of men,
 I pray today for those
 who suffer from split personality
  or other mental affliction;
 who think they are suffering
  from an incurable disease;
 who are readier to resign themselves
  to their sickness than to you.
Be their helper, O God!

O Father of us all,
 bless the children of this land,
 and grant that they may never lack
 love and guidance.
Let family life be pure and happy.
Bless those whose work is mainly in the home,
  those who rarely get the limelight,
  those who feel weary or useless.
Give them to know, O loving God,
 that you reward them according to
  faithfulness,
 not according to earthly fame.
Hear my prayer, O gracious One,
 for those who seek peace among the
  nations;
 for those who live in conditions
  where it is rather hard to be good;
 for those who suffer from sadness.

Now give your blessing, Lord,
 to those who have made mistakes
 and are truly sorry for them.
May they walk—and may I walk—
 further along the road to your likeness.
And may we all finally arrive!

Amen.

VII

Today, Lord, there will be many
 who are seriously ill or grief-stricken.
Hear me as I pray for them,
 that they may know your fatherly care
 for them.
May your healing presence be with them—
 known or unknown to them.
May doctors and nurses know
 that their skill and their sympathy
 are all a part
 of your wonderful pattern of redemption.

Give fresh courage and hope
 to those who say 'it's no use trying'.
Bless those who are living
 lives without purpose,
 lives without power.
Reveal yourself, O God,
 to those who know so little
  of your love or your life;
 to those who cannot or will not
  see the light as it is in Jesus.
Speak, O Lord, to all those
 who are self-centred;
 may they learn kindliness.
Speak, O Lord, to all those
 who are bitter;
 may they learn to love and forgive.

Bless those who feel they are
 too sinful ever to be forgiven—
 and may they discover you
 as the all-forgiving Father.
And if life for some has little music in it,
 put a song in their lips, O God!

Amen.

THE FELLOWSHIP OF SUFFERING

I

O Father, I know you wish evil on no man.
As I come before you with gratitude for your
guarding me against the ravages of evil, I
remember that there are many for whom these
days will be but a succession of trials and cares.
Hear my prayer, Lord, for those who are going
through the valley of the shadow;
who are held captive by infirmity;
who are in the midst of any kind of suffering or
misery.
Bless them as you have blessed me.

As part of the fellowship of suffering,
I am aware, Lord, you can use my prayers
as a channel of blessing to others.
Be with those this day who suffer
from loneliness and friendlessness;
from depression and inadequacy;
from disillusionment and deception.
Reveal yourself in your great power
to the poor and the despairing;
to the weak and the helpless;
to the sick and the refugee.
And if you can use me to bring healing and
comfort, here I am, O Lord!

O Christ, the healer of men and women, of boys
and girls, may your healing touch be felt today
by those who know little of true wholeness.
May any who seek only physical wholeness
be prompted to seek also wholeness of soul!
And may those who blame you for their
suffering or sorrow come to realise that you
desire their health and their joy! Amen.

II

O God, you have given me to share
in the mysterious fellowship of suffering;
and so I pray now for those
who do not have the faith
and the sense of wellbeing that I have.
Bless those who have been pronounced incurable.
Bless those from whom all hope has gone.
Bless those who have been shattered by
misfortune.
Let those who are desperately lonely or are full of
self-pity feel the touch of your love for them.
Let those who are fearful and fretting
find your peace.
Let all men know, with the Psalmist,
not only that the afflictions
of the righteous are many,
but that the Lord can deliver them
from each and every one!

Whenever I can bring a measure of comfort or
offer my friendship, let me not be slow to be
an instrument of your healing.
O you who are the compassionate one, make me
more 'feeling' and loving as I live in your world.
Help me to identify myself with the troubles and
griefs of others.

O lover of my soul, let me see that
in loving others, I love you.
O servant of the world, let me see that
in serving others, I serve you.
Let men turn more readily to you for strength of
heart, O source of healing power!
Let men turn more readily to you for buoyancy of
spirit, O source of liberating joy!

Amen.

III

O God, eternal and almighty, who in Christ your
 Son endured the suffering of the Cross, let men
 everywhere be aware how precious is the
 salvation you have gained for them!
O Saviour, let your wounds be men's healing!
O Saviour, let your Cross be their deliverance!
O Saviour, let your death be their life!

It is of your nature, O God,
 to transform darkness into light;
 to answer human tragedy with divine triumph.
With the consciousness of your care of me, I come
 to you now, Lord, with the needs of others on
 my heart.
Bless those who suffer grievous pain,
 and are heavily handicapped by weakness.
Bless those whose recovery is so long delayed
 that they are growing impatient
 and becoming deeply depressed.
In you, O Saviour, may men
 find refreshment for their bodies;
 find repose for their minds;
 find rest for their souls.

You, Lord, have revealed yourself as one who
 desires our fullest health—health of body,
 mind, and soul.
Let us all seek that wholeness
 which is your gift to those
 who are in tune with you.
But if we cannot meanwhile
 have that harmony and that wholeness,
 let us nevertheless continue to seek it,
 in the hope that, in due time,
 the vision will become the reality.

Amen.

IV

O Lord my God, you are the healer
of men's bodies and souls—
even though many people don't realise it.
Raise them, Lord, to a clearer vision
of your renewing power,
helping them to resign themselves
not to their illness, but to *you*—
knowing that you are the God of
compassion.
Guide those who shall minister
to the sick today,
and if my prayers can help any who are ill,
grant that I may not be slow
to offer such prayers in your name.

Friend of all, I pray for those who I know are lonely.
Father of all, I pray for those who I know
feel insecure.
Forgiver of all, I pray for those who I know
feel guilty.

Lord, bless those who suffer from blindness.
As they pray for light for the body, may they be
thankful for the light of the soul.
Bless those who suffer from dumbness.
As they pray for the opening of their mouths, may
they be thankful for the opening of their hearts.
Bless those who suffer from deafness.
As they pray for the gift of hearing, may they be
thankful for that inner voice which they've
heard in their souls.
Now give me the spirit of sympathy,
so that I may think as others think
and feel as others feel.
And to you, O healing spirit,
I shall ever give praise and glory. Amen.

V

Today, O God, I fervently pray that you will be with the sick—especially those who feel that their ailment makes them exiles from the love of their fellows.
I pray you to be with the homeless,
and with those in unhappy homes;
with the friendless and lonely;
with the despairing and the hopeless.
Minister your love to them, O God—
through me or through others
who acknowledge you as Saviour and Lord.

O spirit of creation, grant men strength
for the weakness of their bodies.
O spirit of truth, grant men resolution
for the discords of their minds.
O spirit of life, grant men refreshment
for the aridness of their souls!

Lord, may I always be readier
to bear the burdens of others
than to complain about my own,
to enter into the experiences of others
than to fence myself in, to be a part
of the fellowship of suffering
than to enjoy a life of smooth sailing.
In all the relationships of daily life
let me take really seriously
the duty of loving—not just tolerating—
one another.
Let me never forget that,
in your gracious providence and plan,
my prayers—and my deeds—
can play a real part in the accomplishing
of your healing purpose for my fellows.
Amen.

VI

There are many, O God, who live
in the belief that this earthly life
is all that there is—
and that it is without meaning.
Reveal the measure of your timeless love
to such as these,
and bring them something of the peace
which you have brought to me.
May your gracious spirit bless those who mourn or grieve for dear ones—and help them to lay hold on the gospel of hope.
I pray too for homeless children and for children who live in homes where there is very little love.
Prosper the efforts of those who seek
to help such young ones,
and may these children still,
by the wonder of your loving providence,
find Him who is friend of all.

Grant to all sufferers, O Lord,
the comfort of your life.
Grant to all sinners, Lord,
the cleansing of your life.
Grant to all seekers, Lord,
the completeness of your life.

Bless those, Lord, who are
confined to bed with sickness,
and give them a desire not just
for renewal of body but of soul too!
Bless those who are in constant pain,
and bring to them liberty and peace.
Bless those who have become physically ill through disharmony of soul, and bring them pardon and renewal of spirit.
For Jesus' sake. Amen.

VII

You, Lord, have given to most of us the urge to
 wholeness, and have assured us your own will is
 'life and good for all of mortal breath'.
Sometimes our sicknesses cannot be healed
 because humans don't yet know enough;
 but let men be in no doubt
 that your healing power is ever available—
 if we can only harness it to our needs!
Knowing, O God, that your will is
 for your people to be whole,
I pray today in confidence
 for those lying on beds of pain;
 for those living under the shadow of sorrow;
 for those desperately seeking relief.
Preserve them from the temptation
 of accepting their trouble as 'your will'.
Help them to see that
 what *may* be hindering their healing
 is their too ready submission—
 and their too slow cooperation.

O physician of men, give the grace of wisdom
 to all doctors and surgeons.
O lover of men, give the grace of tenderness
 to all who watch over the sick.
O sanctifier of men, give the grace of holiness
 to all ministers of your word.

Grant, O God of power and of love, that all those
 in the nadir of experience may have the
 confident hope of being in the heights once
 again.
And may I myself be given a deeper spirit of
 concern for others, and a deeper faith in your own
 promise to 'arise with healing in your wings'!
Amen.

THE CHURCH AND THE WORLD

I

Things aren't happening as fast
  as I would like, Lord!
I'd like to see the Church
  making more of an impact.
I'd like to see my own witness
  pulling in more converts for you, Lord!
But I'm trying to remember
  that the harvest *is* promised—
  to those who don't lose heart.
Your Church hardly seems to *expect*
  conversions nowadays, Lord!
Give her a new sense of expectancy.
Give her a new sense of power.
And let your saving work among men
  Go on unabated—and unashamed.

O you who are king and head of the Church,
  may my own membership be loyal and
    meaningful.
May I live to see the Church being
    'successful'
  in her mission to add daily to her numbers.
May your Church never compromise
  with the truth to which she witnesses.
May those who are 'sitting on the fence'
  stir themselves to fight the good fight.

May I myself be a good advertisement
  for the Christian way of life.
Give to me a real sense of being a member
  not just of the local church,
  but of your Body,
  so that your cause may flourish—
    now and always. Amen.

II

Eternal God, who can bind us all
  into a strong and dedicated force for good,
  forbid that your Church shall be silent
  when there is social injustice.
Forbid that your Church shall be known
  as a self-preservation society!
In these challenging days give her courage
  to dare any consequence of being true to you.
Let her have a greater readiness
    to tune herself to your voice;
    to take your word really seriously;
    to test her work and witness.
And may yours be the glory and praise!

Grant in these days, Lord,
  that your Church may find a new conviction
  of your dwelling in the midst of her—
  and may I be one of her most loyal
  and devout members!
May your Church be in the forefront
  of the crusade against evil in all its forms.
Let those with wealth and influence
  use these gifts responsibly.
Revive your work, Lord, in our nation.

Lord, you need people with a sense of
    mission;
  not just evangelists, but social workers,
  workers among refugees and the
    underprivileged;
  rescue teams, youth leaders, and the rest.
Give your world such people, Lord—
  people with an urge to lose themselves
  in your service.
And may I be one of them!

Amen.

III

O God, I rejoice today
that I am part of the Church Militant,
and will one day be part
of the Church Triumphant.
Some say there are too many militants
today—
but, alas, not in the Church!
Maybe Churchmen are *too* polite,
too gentle, too ingratiating!
Let your Church be more effective, Lord—
more courageous, more positive,
more optimistic, more loving.

Certainly, Lord, save me from the idea
that the Church is finished!
For how often has your Church languished
and been galvanised into fresh life.
How often individuals have been at a low ebb
and your flood-waters have surged to shore!
And if I myself ever lose
my initial enthusiasm for your cause,
or begin to rest on my laurels,
be quick, Lord, to stir me up again!

Save me, O God, from the temptation
to 'hide behind' my Christian profession
and my official connection with the
Church.
May I think larger thoughts
and do nobler deeds,
and may my life be truly geared up
to produce maximum power for the service
of the king and head of the Church.
For His own name's sake.
Amen.

IV

Today, O God, I pray that you may give
 fresh faith and power to your Church,
 so that she may be known—and admired—
 for her fruits.
Put your strength, Lord, into her mind,
 so that she may choose bravely
 and bravely stand by her decisions.
Put your love into her heart,
 so that she may know Christ dwells there.
Put your truth into her mouth,
 so that she may speak of Him
 who is the great hope of the world.

Preserve me, O God, from the temptation
 of thinking I can 'be a good Christian'
 without having anything to do with the
  Church.
Maybe I *can* worship you in the hills,
 or at the lake, or in the garden,
 all by myself, Lord! But *do* I?
Restore to me, and to all of us,
 the realisation that Christianity
 is a religion of fellowship,
 that although my private devotions *are* vital,
 they need the context and the supplement
 of human fellowship with your followers
 and of courageous witness in the community.

Save me, Lord, from that unhealthy loneliness
 which often leads to a false sense of values.
Save me, Lord, from that exaggerated
 individualism which often leads to a perverted
 outlook on life.
Save me, Lord, from that perilous self-concern
 which can often lead to the destruction of my
 real self. Amen.

V

Eternal God, you who have given your Church
the task and the joy
of helping to bring in your kingdom,
I readily fulfil today your desire
that I pray for its coming.
And if the Church is tempted to despair
that there aren't more signs of its dawning,
let her remember those of her members
in whom it *has* dawned—and I'm one of
them!

In these days of challenge and stress
may your Church find a greater readiness
to lose her life for your dear sake—
and so actually *find* it.
Give your Church tolerance and patience.
Give her something of your life and love.
And forbid that she shall turn in on herself
and so be hindered from knowing your will.

In her worship and service of you, Lord,
may the Church have singleness of purpose,
never succumbing to the temptation
of wanting the best of 'two worlds',
but loving and serving only you.
Save her from the error
of making prayer a substitute for action,
from the smooth lips that utter brave words
which do not become brave deeds.
Bless, O Lord, those who preach Christ
in the distant places of the earth,
and strengthen those who witness for you
in this our own dear land.
And all for Christ's own sake.
Amen.

VI

This day, O God, I pray you
to bless your Church and to help her always
to seek to preach News more than views.
Give her joy in mediating your blessings
and in being an agent for reconciliation
in a world of stress and division.
And in some small way may I myself
be a mediator and an agent in this great
task.

May your Church throb with new vitality,
and may she not only expect great things
but attempt great things
to the glory of your holy name.
Match men to their tasks,
however formidable those tasks seem to be;
and give to all members of your Church
the faith to do what lies to hand
with a real sense of mission.
Let the Church have a deep conviction
of the ultimate triumph
of good over evil,
of right over wrong—
and give *me*, Lord, the urge to play a part
in the achieving of that same triumph.

O you who are the life,
help your Church to absorb it.
O you who are the truth,
help your Church to acknowledge it.
O you who are the way,
help your Church to walk in it.

And now may I myself always be 'in the game'
instead of 'on the fence'—
and may yours be the glory for ever.
Amen.

VII

O God, my strength and shield,
you who send forth your followers
into the many-sided discipline of life,
I thank you for the tasks which daily test
the courage and loyalty of your Church.
May she always be more anxious
to overcome circumstances than to deplore
them;
to respond to discipline than to fret under it;
to forge ahead than to take things easy.

May my own membership of the Church,
Lord,
be more dynamic and more meaningful.
Let me never hold back from witnessing
because of false humility or diffidence.
Let me *want* to 'become involved'
with the Church—and with the world—
remembering it's my privilege as well as duty
to be a light to others who know you not.

I know, Lord, the Church is your Body—
or should be!
May she never be just a social club.
May she never be just a spiritual refuge.
Praise be to you, O God,
for the Church's witness through the ages,
and for the opportunity you have given us
to carry on the torch of faith.
Now grant that your Church today may always
put your word before her opinions,
put your cause before her reputation,
put your glory before her 'success'.

And let my own joy always be in you
who are king and head of the Church!
Amen.

I

O Lord of life, I acknowledge
  the 'little miracle of resurrection'
  which brings me from sleep to consciousness.
Your pattern for my physical life, Lord,
  is indeed wonderful.
But I rejoice even more in the pattern you have
  made for the life of the spirit.
Help me even now to claim with gratitude
  your offer of eternal life;
  and may I find that this faith
  will transform the life
  which I live here and now.
Keep me alive to the joy and thrill
  of living and serving in your world—
  and grant that I may always regard myself
  as a pilgrim, not a wanderer.
Grant me that longing
  for the perfection of your likeness in me,
  which is your promise to the redeemed.

Help me to ponder the life of Christ,
  and to enter more deeply into it.
Help me to ponder the death of Christ,
  and to die more really to sin.
Help me to ponder the resurrection of Christ,
  and to rise afresh with Him.

And I thank you, Father, for those who,
  having lived faithful lives on earth,
  have entered into the kingdom
  where deep calls to deep.
Keep the memory of their lives before me,
  and nourish in me that faith
  which looks to our re-uniting. Amen.

II

Lord, help me more and more to rejoice
  in you as the deepest reality of my life,
  and remove those barriers
  which hinder my communion with you.
You are the gracious spirit
  upholding and blessing me day by day,
  and I rejoice that you have opened my
    heart
  to the message of eternal love.
By your power, Lord, I live on this earth
  as one whose true home is heaven.
May I always seek to make the present
  my continual opportunity
  of preparing for the future—
  and in this preparedness may I live,
  and die.

I thank you for the communion of saints,
  and for the memory of loved ones;
    for the hope of immortality;
    for the victory of the risen Christ.
May I never imagine that life consists
  in how much I have
  or in how long I live.
Make me more interested in quality
  than in quantity!

O God, my creator and father,
  redeem and strengthen the life I live,
  so that the love of my heart,
      the thoughts of my mind,
      the works of my hands
  may be a worthwhile offering to you,
  and I shall feel it a life well lived.
And so I commit all the coming hours to you,
  O bestower of life eternal! Amen.

III

Thank you, Lord, for giving me
  the consciousness of your life
  surging in and around me.
How can I praise you enough
  for letting me share in your life?
For though I am nothing in myself,
  you have made me immortal!
Though I am powerless in myself,
  you have made me strong!
May I more frequently be alive
  in your life,
  and aflame with your fire,
  seeking to commune with you
  and to be used by you
  in the hallowing of your name.

Help me, eternal one, now and always
  to see beyond the disharmony
  and the dispeace of the world
  to the pattern of unity and concord,
  and to the fulfilment of your promise
  to draw all men to yourself.
Forbid that I shall try to hide *from* glory,
  but may always head *for* glory!

And so I would renew my trust in you
  as my risen Lord, O Christ.
I would proclaim afresh my faith in you
  as conqueror of death.
I would give thanks again
  for bringing me into touch
  with that eternal life
  of which your word speaks.
May others be brought into touch with it
  as a result of meeting me!

Amen.

IV

O Saviour Christ, I thank you
  that you have consecrated,
  by your Rest in the tomb,
  the graves of all believers;
And I praise you for my dear ones
  who have now entered
  into the promise of eternal life.
In the light of your rising again,
  forbid, O Christ my Lord,
  that I should become 'materially-minded',
  or that I should be satisfied
  with any kind of life other than that
  which is your purpose for me.

May the power of your rising
  surge mightily through me, O Christ,
  and by the same power, Lord,
    turn my every doubt to assurance;
    turn my every sorrow to joy;
    turn my every fear to quiet repose.
Your promise of eternal life
  gives me the best possible 'prospects'!
But let me never forget
  that the eternal can—and does—
  break into the present!

I come to you today, O God,
  because you have made me for yourself,
  and I can find no true rest
  until I find it in you.
In your own time grant me to know
  the blessing of that great company
  who have found true life
  and live with you in eternity.

Amen.

V

This day, O God, I ask you to give me
a reverence for all life,
and to let me live
as those who have been redeemed.
O you who give yourself to me,
help me to give myself to you.
O you who seek to possess me,
help me to *want* to be possessed.

How good it is, O Lord my God,
to know your saving power is active *now*.
Yet I thank you too
that you have marked me
for the day of my final liberation!
In the meantime, keep alive in me
the sacred longing
to be like Jesus my Saviour.
May life for others be sweeter
because of the song I sing.
May life for others be purer
because of the love I bear.
And if any of your people
draw near to death this day,
let them with serenity and with hope
commit their spirits to you, O God.

I rejoice again that you are the God
not of the dead, but of the living.
Your own creative life comes to me daily
through your great and invisible spirit—
and I thank you for the sense of uplift
and the sense of wellbeing
which I have found through him.
Let all your people think more
of their destiny than of their descent!

Amen.

VI

Thank you, Lord, for giving me patience
  as I make my great but slow pilgrimage
  to the kingdom of light and peace,
  and for giving me the assurance
  that those who wait patiently for you
  shall possess the land.
Praise be yours, O Lord,
  that I can leave the issues of each day
  confidently in your hands,
  in the knowledge that I and my loved ones
  are in your safe keeping.

Bless those, O God,
  who are 'hopelessly' adrift on life's seas—
  and give them hope.
Bless those, O God,
  who know even now,
  the hell of separation from you—
  and give them a glimpse of heaven.
Bless those, O God,
  who think life is a tragedy—
  and give them the seeds of victory.

Lord, even when I lie down to sleep
  you are at my right hand,
  and you sustain my life.
I know that heaven is about my bed
  as well as above the pathways I walk.
I know that, awake or asleep,
  I cannot be separated from your love.
But help me in these waking hours
  to be *fully* aware of my amazing destiny,
  to be *fully* alive to the glory
    and to the opportunity
    of living each day with you.

Amen.

VII

By your great power, eternal God,
  I can live with Christ my Saviour,
  here on earth and in eternity.
Thanks be to you, heavenly Father,
  for my confidence that your love is with me
  in the hours of each day.
You will work through my faults and my fears
  and bring me to the desired haven.
May I know, then, O God, before this day draws
  to its close, that you have taken firmer hold of
  me and that I have taken firmer hold of you—
  for in this knowledge lies the sweetest
  benediction.

Help me in these days of my flesh, Lord, to enjoy
  the things of earth, but not to set my whole
  heart on them; to become a little more aware of
  my citizenship in heaven—but not to depreciate
  or despise my citizenship here upon earth.
Let me ever seek my End in you,
  the giver of eternal life.
Amid every pleasure and sorrow,
  amid every hope and fear,
  let me remember the incorruptible
    inheritance
  which awaits me.

Thank you, Saviour Christ,
  for those whom I knew on earth
  and who have already entered
    into this inheritance.
Now may I live constantly in the knowledge
  that you are with me always,
  and that my loved ones
  are in your safe and gracious keeping.
Amen.